THE
BLUFFER'S GUIDE®
TO
TEACHING

NICK YAPP

Oval Books

Published by Oval Books
335 Kennington Road
London SE11 4QE
United Kingdom

Telephone: +44 (0)20 7582 7123
Fax: +44 (0)20 7582 1022
E-mail: info@ovalbooks.com
Web site: www.ovalbooks.com

First published by Ravette Publishing, 1987
Reprinted/updated: 1989, 1991, 1992, 1993,
1994, 1996, 1997, 1998

New edition published by Oval Books, 1999
Updated 2000, reprinted 2001

Series Editor – Anne Tauté

Cover designer – Jim Wire, Quantum
Printer – Cox & Wyman Ltd
Producer – Oval Projects Ltd

The Bluffer's Guides® series is based
on an original idea by Peter Wolfe.

The Bluffer's Guide®, The Bluffer's Guides®,
Bluffer's®, and Bluff Your Way®
are Registered Trademarks.

ISBN: 1-902825-98-5

CONTENTS

A HISTORY LESSON

Background

Teaching is an old and vaguely honourable profession dating back thousands of years. In that time there have been six famous teachers: Plato, Aristotle, Jesus, Dr Quelch, Mr Chips and David Blunkett.

Recent commentators on education have suggested that teaching standards are falling. This may well be true since David Blunkett is not generally regarded as highly as Plato.

There is no mention of any school in the Bible. People then had other and cruder ways of persecuting each other. The Greeks did have schools, ramshackle open-air affairs where the teachers were constantly having to take hemlock. The NUT put a stop to all that, but there are signs that the practice may soon be revived. The Romans also had schools, but became confused and called their teachers 'magistrates' and their pupils 'disciples'. It didn't really matter as slaves did the work of both. There are signs that this practice may also soon be revived.

In the late 19th century, laws were passed making attendance at school compulsory for children. Schools thus joined prisons and mental asylums as the only places where people could be sent against their will. The thrust of all educational reform has been to have more children sent to more places for longer.

The first schools in Britain were draughty, cold, ill-equipped set-ups which have survived for thousands of years and are all called King Edward's School. The schools of today are no longer prison-like – none of them are sufficiently solidly built – and are named after the less romantic socialists of the period 1945-69.

The last 15 years have seen such radical reforms

that all sorts of wild rumours now circulate regarding education. Like all rumours in education you disregard these at your peril.

Teaching Today

In the 'Good Old Days' (the late 1960s and early 1970s) becoming a teacher was relatively simple. You had to be able to: a) write your name; and b) stand unaided.

And, once you were in, it was almost impossible to have you removed because it is impossible to prove just how bad any teacher is. This is vital information that you must remember all the time. It is the light that shines in the darkness of a wet November afternoon with 4F or the Third Year non readers. It is the one advantage that teaching has over other professions such as Radioactive Waste Disposal or Whaling, or Sweeping Motorways.

The Good Old Days, of Open Plan Classrooms, the Discovery Method, De-Schooling and Denim Jacketed Freaks, have given way to the Age of the National Curriculum. It is still almost impossible to be sacked from teaching unless you've had something to do with Preaching World Revolution After You've Been Told Not To, or Grand Larceny of School Property (we're talking lorry loads of stationery here), but you can now be made redundant at the drop of a mortarboard. This is a result of one of the Laws of Educational Economics – the more money spent on education, the fewer the teachers, the bigger the classes.

The problem with teaching is not so much can you get a job, but can you ever change it once you've got it. All the more reason, therefore, to think carefully about:

What Sort of School?

This depends on what sort of forms you like completing. Teachers still spend much of their day in the classroom, but now spend all their evenings filling out forms. There are several sorts of school and several sorts of form. Starting with the smallest (of both), and excluding Day Nurseries, usually under the control of the Local Health Authority, there are **Nursery Schools** (3- to 5-year-old pupils), **Infant Schools** (5- to 7-year-olds), **Junior Schools** (7- to 11-year-olds), **Secondary Schools** (11- to 18-year-olds) and **City Technology Colleges** (11- to 18-year-olds). Some Authorities became very muddled in the 1960s, and opened what they called **Middle Schools**, for pupils from 9 to 13 years. Nobody knows why. Lots of things in teaching happen like that.

Nursery Schools are good because the children are very young and small and wonderfully uninhibited in their approach to the outside world, of which school is their first glimpse. They have wide-eyed respect for teachers, and their parents are overjoyed to find someone who will take their offspring away for a few hours a day without charge. So, it's all smiles and co-operation and hardly a cross word. The drawbacks are that the children are so young that you have to teach them absolutely everything except how to be sick, which they are most of the time. Much of the day is spent wiping away tears (theirs), and snot, and tying shoelaces.

Infant Schools are good because the tears are less frequent, and teaching is a bit easier and can be exciting. Teachers get the chance to introduce children to the delights of paper weaving, sorting shapes and beadwork. There is also the thrill of making pictures by sticking bits of pasta and lentils on to sugar paper. Modern technology has yet to devise a glue that will attach macaroni to paper for longer than 20 minutes, but good teachers never let that get them down. Other

7

good points about Infant Schools are that parents are still co-operative, and children still respect their teachers. The main drawback is other Infant teachers, whose conversation tends to dwell on carpets and curtain material. A small drawback is that children still can't tie their shoelaces. It takes a very long time to tie the shoelaces of a whole class, and by the time you get to the last, the first five have experimented and untied theirs again.

Junior Schools are good because some of the children have learned to read, so you may not have to go through the Ladybird Much Loved Tales for the three hundred and fourth time. Children at Junior School achieve a measure of independence in their work. They can write, and cut out shapes, and use glue, and 'if they are sensible' stand outside the school gates and do a traffic census. Vast amounts of closely detailed, highly localised and very inaccurate information are gathered in this way every year by every Junior School. The information is of minimal importance, but it does provide data for Bar Graphs. Bar Graphs in Junior Schools are like Government White Papers in Education; they prove that something is happening, even if nobody knows what.

The drawbacks in Junior Schools are record-keeping, Fourth Year Pupils (who are very full of themselves and terrified of going on to Secondary Schools), and the lack of openings for promotion (unless you want to accept responsibility for everything from Computer Security to Cross-Curricular Strategies), and Literacy and Numeracy Hours.

If you are lucky, the Head won't worry unduly about how well you perform your special tasks, but will view promotion simply as a way of rewarding a valued teacher with a bit more money – about enough for another bottle of gin a week. This approach is sadly declining. These days, a 'Post of Responsibility' can mean that you won't even have time to drink that extra bottle of gin. Another drawback in Junior Schools is that more than a few children are beginning to exhibit what are called **Special Needs**, the theory which goes beyond the notion that some children have poor eye/motor co-ordination and can't tie their own shoelaces.

Secondary Schools are good because you get Marking and Preparation Periods (never call them 'Free', the real world may get to hear of it). This means you can sit in the staffroom and legitimately read *The Guardian*. Secondary Schools are also good because children are constantly going out of your lessons for Play Rehearsals or Careers Advice or Remedial Reading or to see the Head of Pastoral Care for a right old rollicking. And there are more chances of promotion in Secondary Schools. The drawbacks, however, are considerable.

First, there are the children – they're bigger than you. You may not think this matters: they do. They're all bored and sophisticated, and some are totally disillusioned. Then there are the parents, who cling tenaciously to the belief that the chronic ineptitude and multitudinous shortcomings of their children are your fault. Lastly, there are the Senior Staff, who call each other by their first names and keep going into little huddles whence they emerge with heart-stopping plans for reorganising the school to your disadvantage. Secondary School can be a very tough existence and you may spend a lot of the time wiping away tears (yours).

Special Education

Some teachers, like some children, have 'special educational needs', which used to be better met in one of the many branches of Special Education set up by the 1944 Education Act (What Rab Butler Saw). This empowered Local Education Authorities to set up a variety of Special Schools:

- Physically Handicapped
- Educationally Sub Normal
- Delicate
- Maladjusted, etc.

It was a very good idea and it was surprising that it lasted so long – good ideas don't usually last long in education. It has all come to an end now, by virtue of the 1981 Education Act (Joseph and His Amazing Technological Dream) and a slurry of other bits of legislation that has engulfed schools since.

Children with Special Needs are now catered for in mainstream schools. They have ceased to be labelled 'delicate', 'ESN' or 'maladjusted'. They are all children with problems. It is becoming increasingly difficult to spot the 'special' child when the entire class is swinging from the light sockets, but the Child with Special Needs is usually the one not seeming to enjoy it. His or her teacher tells another teacher who says something ought to be done. Two terms later, someone tells the Head. Two years later the Head tells the Educational Psychologist. The Educational Psychologist says it's really a question of giving the child time to settle down.

When the school is on the point of collapse and the Special Needs Child is letting off the fire alarm daily, biting people in Assembly, and, more to the point, has damaged the Educational Psychologist's car, the Inspector is called in. The Inspector panics (it's what Inspectors do best) and the Parents are summoned to the school where an argument breaks out about a) what's wrong, and b) whose fault it is. And all the time this is happening EVERYBODY WRITES EVERYTHING DOWN.

In exceptional circumstances somebody has the temerity to ask what is going to be done, but once everything has been written down, most authorities are satisfied that enough has already been done.

All concerned now examine their positions. The Parents have Rights. The Authority has Obligations. The Educational Psychologist has a damaged car (and a mobile phone). The Head (appropriately) has Headaches. The Teacher has Nothing, except a child who is finding increasingly inventive ways of being identified. By means of a series of meetings, detailed reports are compiled. These reports are called (appropriately) **FAs**.

It is envisaged that at some point all the parties involved will suddenly become of like mind and inspiration, as though on some coach trip on the Road to Damascus: a solution will be found. The simple practice is that Parents never agree to anything and Special Needs Children are **statemented** and stay right where they are.

Private Schools

If none of the above appeals, there is always the last refuge of the scoundrel – Private Education. Private Schools range from trendy centres of excellence with prize-winning string quartets, electron microscopes and their own helicopters, to Dickensian hell holes which even the **DFEE*** condemns.

Teaching in a Private School is very different. Children there wear caps and short trousers and call male teachers 'Sir' to their faces but give them unflattering nicknames like 'Rustyballs' and 'Randy Mac' behind their backs. Or they wear berets and pleated skirts and call the women teachers by their real

*Department for Education & Employment – earlier departments apparently being against education and employment.

11

names to their faces and worship them behind their backs.

To get a job in a private school you need an impressive CV. The jobs are advertised in quality newspapers, but some desperate souls go to educational agencies, who find them 'positions' in the Welsh mountains or on the Isle of Islay. It can be very creepy.

SCHOLARIS PERSONAE

Most of the time teachers lurk in a world inhabited only by other teachers, even at parties. But, just as it takes a multitude of talents to produce the US Space Shuttle or the Eurovision Song Contest, so there are lots of non teachers involved in Education.

Heads

Heads are the most obvious non teachers, since they spend all their time as far away from children as possible. Heads wear suits (male and female) and do four things:
1. Take Assembly
2. Design complicated Timetables
3. Juggle the School's Finances (see **LMS**).
4. Worry about Litter.

Governors

Governors are worthy citizens, some of them appointed by the respectable political parties (the ones allowed to do commercials on television) and some co-opted from other spheres of education. There are all sorts of Governors and they all have different roles:

a) The Role of the Parent Governor is to embarrass the other governors by showing off either how much they know about education, or how little.
b) The Role of the Political Governor is to argue with the other political governors about PPPs, Housing, Grants, Hiring of Halls, Local Facilities for the Elderly – anything, so long as it's not to do with Education.
c) The Role of the Teacher Governor is to make sure that any discomfort the Head experiences at a Governors' Meeting is increased.

Administrators

Administrators are very dull people who sit in very dull offices and make life virtually intolerable for teachers because they believe that teachers are making life intolerable for them. Try not to meet them.

Inspectors

Traditionally there were two types of Inspector – **HMIs** (State) and **LEAs** (local), neither of which was to be trusted. The first had the grace to be infrequent visitors, scuttling into schools every five or six years to have a 'quick word' (sherry) with the Head. If they turned up more frequently, or came in numbers, it meant trouble: someone had grassed about the Staff Bridge Club which met during Assembly, or someone had noticed that no child in the school could read.

Local Inspectors were kinder and almost motherly. This was because they didn't want to castigate a school run by their own employers. They would suggest just one or two "little points" needed attention then drone on for hours about record keeping. A visit from a Local Inspector rarely meant trouble.

Nowadays they always come in numbers and it does mean trouble. They are not there to make sure a school runs efficiently and offers a good education. They are there, backed by the *Daily Mail,* to make teachers quake. The weeks before, during and even after an **Ofsted** inspection are the worst in any teacher's career.

There is only one thing to do when you are the subject of an inspection – keep asking the inspectors to demonstrate. "Show me how to separate the knife-fighters in 4 delta." "Show me how to hear one child read while supervising the other 42." "Show me how to run a science department with a budget that wouldn't support a fasting hermit."

Advisory Teachers

These are people who have had one good idea which they've shared with their Inspector. To be an Advisory Teacher appears at first sight to be a jolly good wheeze. You get paid for driving from school to school telling other people what to do while never actually having to try your red hot idea on the children. But God has decreed that no-one in Education should have it that good, and there are several drawbacks:

a) You have to organise In-Service Training: and if you thought German novels or Polish films were tedious, try Teachers' Courses.
b) You have to spend a lot of time with your Inspector.
c) Every teacher you meet will secretly or openly hate you because you are such a smart-arse.

School Secretaries

School Secretaries are the most important people in Education. They know where everything is; which forms to fill in for injuries, riots, pay, ordering equipment; how to add and balance dinner money; how to deal with annoying and unwelcome callers. They are even prepared to spend time listening to former pupils who have dropped in for a visit because they have just been sacked from work. You get on the wrong side of the School Secretary at your peril.

Schoolkeepers

It is impossible to get on the right side of the schoolkeeper, but you have to remember that he (it is always 'he') and his Alsatian are the most powerful duo in the school. Schoolkeepers have grasped better than anyone else that the main aim in education is to make other people's lives difficult. They have perfected the art of creating a different climatic region for each part of the school, so that while one wilts in tropical fever heat, another freezes in arctic chill. They instinctively know which rooms to lock (the ones you want to use) and which to leave open to passing snatch thieves (the ones you left valuables in). They order vast stocks of hard lavatory paper so the school has years of suffering to look forward to. They can destroy, at a stroke, any display that you've sweated over for weeks.

Schoolkeepers can never be faulted. If you criticise or attack them, you will be met by the grim-faced announcement that he's "put in a req". This means that somewhere there is a piece of paper, like an indulgence, that absolves him from all blame. The next thing you know, your classroom has lost its heating, the staffroom coffee has disappeared, there is no soap in the staff loos and there's a skip full of rusting metal and rotting wood in your parking space.

Attendants

There are two sorts of School Attendant – the Wonderful and the Awful. Wonderful Attendants look after wounds and woes, find equipment you need, read to fidgety children, make hot drinks, and generally bring sunshine into a school. Awful Attendants act like Bette Davis in *Whatever Happened to Baby Jane?* Your main concern, however, is:

Teachers

These come in all shapes, sizes, ages, political persuasions and degrees of literacy, but there are three main types.

1. **White Collar Teachers** who dress smartly (hoping for promotion), attend Courses, read Committee Reports ('hi-lighting' bits and making notes in the margins), know the right people, and command discipline. They become Heads of Department or Deputy Heads sickeningly quickly, and go on to become Heads. They are awesome, but do not worry about how to relate to them. They never relate to anybody.

2. **Blue Collar Teachers** who dress in very old cardigans, shiny suits whose lapels have withered and curled at the points, or worn woollies and skirts. They sit in *their* corner of the staffroom, roll cigarettes, drink gallons of coffee, are first to the newspaper, and talk about ex-pupils who left 17 years ago, or new cars. They teach Home Economics or Metalwork, which they stubbornly refuse to call Craft, Design and Technology. They command discipline because they are fierce and have Workshop Rules to fall back on. They are easy to relate to, as there is no malice or sense of competition in them, and they are totally sympathetic to your troubles.

16

They are also totally unhelpful.

3. **No Collar Teachers** who dress as though for combat, which is how they approach life. They have strain etched on their faces and stain etched on their jeans. They don't like the Head, the school, the children, each other, their Union (though vociferously present at all its meetings), most foreign governments, *all* British governments, and especially the way England played in the last International – it doesn't seem to matter which sort. They command discipline because they are always so angry. They make friendly overtures towards you before coming to despise you because you are bourgeois.

There is, of course, a fourth type of teacher, and that is YOU – sensitive, conscientious, broadminded, sincere and professional. You dress in whatever you find that is reasonably clean, constantly lose your timetable, never seem to arrive anywhere on time and can't command discipline. Nor can you ever work out if your pay slip is right.

Being More Professional

'Being more professional' is a phrase that is constantly bandied about though no-one knows what it means. There are several schools of thought:

a) Teachers wearing ties and turning up on time.
b) Teachers working more than 15 hours a day.
c) Teachers getting less money.
d) Teachers not being ill so much.
e) Teachers throwing all training and experience out of the window and doing only what parents tell them to do.
f) Teachers somehow managing to make their pupils more intelligent.

17

WORKING WITH CHILDREN

Note this phrase – 'working with children'. This is what teachers do most of the time. Teaching is something that happens very, very rarely, but it's nice when it does.

The secret of successful teaching lies in mastering a classroom technique that will keep the children still and quiet. It is one of life's richer ironies that, although you are employed as a teacher, you are judged as a police officer. If the children fail to make any academic progress, that may be passed off as their fault. If they shout, spit, throw things, fight, and run in and out of the classroom, that's your fault.

To guarantee success as a teacher, therefore, you need the charisma of a showbiz megastar and a limitless arsenal of plastic bullets and CS gas. Since nobody knows how to teach classroom management, the only possible approach is a pragmatic one. To which end, the first thing is to know your enemy.

Pupils

There are ten types of pupil – the Good, Bad, Sick, Sickening, Eager, Reluctant, Quick, Slow, Bolshie and Reactionary. All present problems.

1. The Good
Problem: Listen to what you say, know what they're supposed to be doing and do it much too quickly. Constantly thirsting for more education and thereby making you feel guilty and inadequate. *Solution:* Tell them to shut up and think for once about those less fortunate than themselves, who are still struggling to start, let alone complete, the work. This will make *them* feel guilty and inadequate.

2. The Bad

Problem: Can't concentrate, can't sit still, can't do the work, can't keep their mouths shut, can't share, can't leave other children alone. *Solution:* You are not allowed to kill these children, so you have to look around for more devious ways to rid yourself of them. Seeking their suspension or expulsion takes a long time and involves the Head in tricky meetings with parents and governors. A better method is to complain loudly and at length every time you go to the staffroom. Sooner or later one of your more pompous colleagues will say: "Oh, I never have any trouble with him/her" Then you pounce. Play to this monstrous conceit. It should be possible, within half a term at the most, to arrange a transfer. This will relieve you of a troublemaker, and inflate the already swollen ego of your colleague to the extent that he/she might be willing to take another troublemaker next half term.

3. The Sick

Problem: Always limping, sneezing, coughing, vomiting and complaining. *Solution:* Send them to the Attendant with a note, and SEND THEM WITH THE TROUBLE-MAKERS. This way you will get rid of the latter for a few minutes, and the Sick will probably have a bad time on the way to the Attendant. They won't be so ready to be sick next time. This is called Behaviour Modification and is much venerated by Educational Psychologists.

4. The Sickening

Problem: Always grassing, hanging about after school, wanting to help, leaning on you, asking personal questions. *Solution:* Don't try to get rid of them, their resilience is always far greater than yours. When they come to you, sneaking on the other children, get them to write everything down. Stress the importance of this. Say it must go to the Head. Then, when they have written everything down, get them to do it again with punctuation and without spelling mistakes. This is called Child Centred Education, and is also much venerated by Educational Psychologists. It also makes the children give up. When Sickening children lean on you, move suddenly and unexpectedly, so that they fall over. When they bleat about 'helping you', set them onerous, or better, impossible tasks. No treatment is too harsh for such children.

5. The Eager

Problem: Over-enthusiastic. Start on a task before they've half an idea what they're supposed to do. Always want to clean the board, start a class newspaper, put on a puppet show, go on outings to places you would hate to visit. *Solution*: Say "Yes" to everything they suggest, but do nothing. They will soon become as disillusioned and lifeless as the rest of the class.

6. The Reluctant

Problem: Don't want to do anything. Don't want to come to school, learn to read, play, go to the Park, make a picture of a Crusader using crumpled baking foil, have a go on the 'puter', anything. *Solution*: Play on their apathy. Suggest that every task, every activity is too hard, too dangerous, too pointless for them even to consider. They will soon reach a stage of inactivity bordering on the sloth-like. And sloths never present behaviour problems.

7. The Quick

Problem: Can already read, multiply, speak Conversational French, make rock cakes, use a microscope and 'puter', create pictures out of felt shapes, talk about democracy in Zimbabwe, and play the theme from *Superman* on the recorder. *Solution*: They are almost certainly the product of pushy, middle-class parents (probably teachers). Get rid of these children at once. The best way is to praise them to the sky and say to their parents: "I'm afraid the school may not be able to do them justice."

8. The Slow
Problem: You can never move on to the next task as they're never ready for you to wipe the board, turn the page, or start the next worksheet. *Solution*: Once you have got rid of the Quick, and the Trouble-makers, and reduced the Reluctant to paralysis, the Slow don't really present a problem.

9. The Bolshie
Problem: Always want new subjects, new methods, the Perpetual Revolution. Always whiningly aware of what other classes, other schools are doing. "Why can't we have an aquarium/minibus/garden of our own/day trip to Florence?" *Solution*: If they want to get political, you do the same. Talk to them about Market Forces and Cost Effectiveness. That's the way to deal with Bolsheviks.

10. The Reactionary
Problem: Wants to set the clock back a century or two. Whereas the Bolshies are always saying: "Why can't we...?" (The Greedy Revolutionary Syndrome), Reactionaries are always saying: "Why don't you...? (The Lazy Slave Syndrome)... set us proper work/use the cane/give us homework/make us wear uniform?" *Solution*: Point out that their real enemies are the Bolshies, and hope that they'll tear each other to pieces at playtime – as long as you're not on duty.

Class Control

Naturally, the foregoing presents too rosy a picture of life in the classroom and fails to convey the sort of pressure a teacher is under. So here are a few extra 'Do's' and 'Don'ts'.

Do:

1. Talk about the classroom and everything in it as 'my' – my books, my radiator, my chalk, my light bulbs, my broken window catch. The children know this isn't true, and some may want to argue, but children, like animals, respect someone who clearly delineates territorial and proprietorial rights.

2. Enter the classroom noisily, aggressively. The braggarts will be impressed, and the timid will faint clean away.

3. Frequently spend a long time giving the children information that is useless and that they will not understand, but which somehow involves them. For example, pick up the Register and say: "I notice, Dean/Linda/Wayne/Isla, that your attendance is still 2.4 percentile points below the class mean." The children will be quiet because they haven't a clue what it means and they will be wondering if it's good or bad news.

4. Pretend from time to time that you are seized by acute physical pain. This will worry the children and dampen their spirits. Also, you can fill in a great deal of time describing your symptoms. Children love symptoms.

5. Get the biggest bunch of keys you can lay hands on and keep waving it about and banging it on your desk. Children are impressed by keys.

Don't:

1. Wear trainers costing less than £100 a pair, or you'll lose all your street cred.

2. Get involved in anything that may end up in the Court of Human Rights, or, worse, some after-school hours inquiry.

3. Try to treat all the children the same. They'll know you don't mean it, and a bit of well-aimed loathing at one or two can buck some of the others up no end.

4. Ever threaten anything that will involve you in overtime. The children know how unlikely it is that you will carry out that threat.

5. Expect children to be quiet when they watch television or go to the theatre or a concert. Nobody is quiet these days watching television or at the theatre or a concert.

There are also some guaranteed phrases for class discipline: "That boy/girl in the fifth row, fourth column, third desk – bring me that…"/"Would you all like to see some really bad work…?"/"I suppose you're all too young to remember what happened to poor Luckless the last time that was tried…"/"Well, what I said would happen, has happened…"/"Still at it, eh, Stark…?"

Classroom Technique

There are four techniques to be mastered:

1. How to get the children into the classroom.
2. How to keep the children in the classroom.
3. How to get the children out of the classroom.
4. How to deal with the children while they are in the classroom.

1. How to get the children into the classroom

There are still teachers who can line up the children in the corridor, quell them, and march them into the classroom in silence. Alas, such teachers are a dying breed – indeed, some are already dead. In fact, getting children into the classroom doesn't present much of a problem. The end of playtime, the end of Assembly, the beginning of school, any time – in they flock, practically fighting each other to be first. The sad fact is that the playground is such an awful place (protection rackets, fights, up to 20 games of football, sellotape sniffing sessions, etc.) that the children are eager to return to the safety of the classroom.

Much the same is true of the end of Assembly, though this is more an escape from the crippling boredom of the Head's speech on 'Behaviour-at-the-Bus-Stop' or the Deputy Head pretending to know all about Pokémon. The early morning keenness at the beginning of school is so that they can boast to each other about how late they stayed up the night before, watching *Mother Superior Goes Bananas with a Meat Cleaver After Vespers* on video.

2. How to keep children in the classroom

This is also much easier than it used to be. A generation ago children were constantly asking for leave to go to the 'toilet', in reality to sneak off to the boiler room or behind the bike sheds for a quick drag on a well crushed Park Drive or Players No 10. This is no longer a problem: children stay in the classroom and suck ecstasy instead.

3. How to get children out of the classroom

In every class there are, and always have been, those who wish to linger, long after their healthier peers have run screaming down the road to nick anything and everything from the local newsagent and give the elderly residents heart palpitations. These hangers-on want to talk to you. Usually they want to show off, by asking personal questions or being cheeky in front of their mates. Sometimes they want to tell you a joke, usually racist. In all cases they wish to establish what they regard as an atmosphere of chirpy good humour. To combat this, and drive them from the room, you should lead with some doom-laden remark about their sponsored paper chase or their exam prospects. Or you could pretend to know all about Pokémon.

4. **How to deal with children while in the classroom**. This is the very stuff of education. It concerns:

The Curriculum

The Curriculum is to Education what Achelous was to Greek Mythology. It constantly changes its shape, is a thorough nuisance, and you need the resilience and resources of Heracles to master it.

Currently, the Curriculum is described as:

National – A way of making sure that only those subjects for which there are no teachers are taught in schools, i.e. Maths, Physics, Computer Studies.

For Life – Since school-leavers won't get jobs, they have to learn the location of the nearest Social Security Office, Citizens Advice Bureau, Law Centre and Snooker Hall.

Hidden – A trick phrase flung at you during interviews for promotion. Because it's hidden nobody knows where it is or much about it, but a good way of handling it at interview is to say that's what you consider the whole ambience of the school is about.

Traditional – You've got to teach punctuation, spelling and Tables.

Progressive – You've got to teach punctuation, spelling and Tables.

Multi-Ethnic – Being able to say 'Welcome' in a hundred and fifty languages.

Integrated – Lots more staff meetings.

Subjects and Syllabuses

Maths. Amazingly in the age of calculators, computers and credit cards, Maths is still taught in those schools fortunate enough to have a Maths teacher. The main difficulty with teaching Maths is that children either never learn the Four Rules (which is all they need to know) or learn them too quickly, thereby forcing Maths teachers to have to relearn fractions, ratios, LCMs and Venn diagrams, skills about as useful as wild boar hunting or how to make rush dips.

The Numeracy Hour will clearly take care of teaching Maths, as soon as its advocates have worked out an acceptable way of fudging the statistics to prove that it has.

Computer Studies. This keeps the children totally absorbed for hours, as long as they are allowed endless repeats of *Terror Drive to Las Vegas*. Otherwise computers are useless as a teaching aid since the lead with the right Din or Jack plug always disappears, or there are 35 pupils to one computer, or all they want to do is play *Terror Drive to Las Vegas*.

Science. In Infant Science the children discover the properties of water and light and candle wax and are completely enthralled. In Junior Science the children keep tadpoles and discover that Nature excitingly arranges things so that they all die just before they turn into frogs. In Secondary Science the children are unable to behave so all the Bunsen burners and taps are turned off and cupboards kept locked, while the children fill in worksheets and discover nothing.

Design and Technology. Once called woodwork for boys and cooking and sewing for girls, the DFEE has set up **SEAC** (Secondary Examination and Assessment Council) a body whose function is to justify woodwork, cooking and sewing in the curriculum without calling them woodwork, cooking and sewing. This may take several years.

Art. The importance of Art in Education cannot be overstressed as, without Art, there would be nothing for schools to mount, label and stick on walls. The Art syllabus is cleverly arranged so that the amount of praise and encouragement children receive gradually diminishes as their ability increases. Hence the first waxy smears of the four- or five-year-old are greeted with a fulsome delight never again accorded in its learning life. The 15-year old's careful pen and wash study of sea shells and driftwood, on the other hand, is criticised in every detail.

Languages. Years ago children sweated with French and Latin, term after term, poring over incredibly dull texts. Nowadays the thriving Languages Departments don't have textbooks. They have cassettes and videos and brochures and Day Trips and they teach German, Russian, Turkish, Urdu, Punjabi, Arabic, Serbo-Croat, Welsh, Walloon and dozens of other tongues. And yet, plant a Britisher in almost any part of the world and he or she is still lost for words.

27

English and Drama. The difference between an English lesson and a Drama lesson is that in Drama the children are supposed to be running about. Recent educational research has led to the introduction of bold new concepts in the English syllabus, like spelling and learning to read, and a smattering of punctuation. The days of free verse are said to be numbered.

History/Geography/Social Studies/The Humanities/ Environmental Studies/Integrated Studies/Our World. The main threat to this department (apart from its in-built confusion) comes from the Internet. Whatever the subject is called, children know far more about it than their teachers. To function even adequately, you need to be able to whiz round every web site, from www.boffbrain@smartalec.com to www. genibabe@swot.co.yuk.

Home Economics. Strictly speaking this includes Nutrition, Hygiene, Toy Making, Baby Care, and How to Wire a 13 Amp Plug, but all that anybody is interested in is Cooking, so the other branches of the subject are used only as punishments. Most H.E. departments work something of a culinary miracle that puts the Jesus and his loaves and fishes trick to shame. All year the children produce dishes that fall short of scintillating – Baked Apple, Boiled Egg, Toasted Sandwich ('cooking' is interpreted somewhat widely), Open Sandwich, Closed Sandwich, Oat Crunchies. Then, *mirabile dictu*, along comes an Open Day or a Governors' Meeting and suddenly the place erupts in Pavlova, Quiche Normande, Tomatoes à la Grecque – and all made by the children.

Music. Gone are the days of the Tonic Sol-fa (sadly), the *National Song Book,* three descant recorders and Hymn Practice. Gone, too, are the days when every child received instrumental coaching and every Secondary School had its full size Symphony Orchestra, Wind Band, Brass Ensemble, Swing Band, Steel Band and Guitar Group. Music is out. Educational research revealed that playing in a string quartet was no sort of preparation for working in McDonald's, and anyway music was making children happy, and education should have nothing to do with making children (or teachers) happy.

R.E. There was a time when many pundits were convinced that Religious Education was dying out, which seemed a touch ironic since it dealt with the eternal. All this has changed. To prove that there is life hereafter, R.E. has cunningly hitched its wagon to the Multi-Ethnic horse. Now not even atheists can justify withdrawing their offspring from R.E. lessons. The irrefutable arguments in favour of compulsory R.E. are:

a) It introduces children to much of their multi-cultural heritage – suttee, arranged marriages, denial of the right to divorce, public floggings, cutting off hands, All Things Bright and Beautiful, fish teas on Fridays and totally boring Sundays.
b) By studying the lives of Noah, Gandhi, Buddha, Mohammed, and Posh and Beck, children learn the need to be tolerant.
c) It offers fine opportunities for colouring in pictures.
d) It fills tricky gaps in the timetable.

P.E. In the bad old days, P.E. consisted of compulsory competitive games and cold showers. Then came the golden years – Canoeing, Skating, Orienteering, Pot-Holing, Hang Gliding, Unicycling, Mountaineering, Bareback Riding, Microlite Flying, Surfboarding, Synchronised Swimming, and Kick-the-can. All this is

29

old hat now, and P.E. departments are involved in compulsory competitive games – without cold showers: there's no time.

Health Education. Life isn't easy for the Health Education teacher or department, for several reasons:

a) They rely heavily for material (pamphlets, workbooks, wallcharts) on the very institutions whose products they feel they should criticise: the milk marketing board, McDonald's, Tate & Lyle.

b) Expert opinion on what produces good health changes day by day. Yesterday jogging was in, today it's out. Yesterday vegetarians were healthy and wise, today they're heading for early graves. Think of the implications for Sex Education. Yesterday masturbation made you blind, deaf, impotent, stunted and feeble minded – today it may be your best defence against AIDS.

c) H.E. is a very young subject with no historical background so H.E. teachers are forced to run workshops where they hand round questionnaires labelled 'What is Health Education?' Even when they get the questionnaires back, they still don't know.

d) All the children know you shouldn't smoke. All the children know you shouldn't drink, and all pretend they know where babies come from.

Remedial. The days of the Remedial Department and Remedial Education are numbered. Nobody wants to go back to the time when pencils were cut in half (so that Remedial children took *two* lessons to lose a whole pencil), when every transport museum in the land was thronged with 'under-achievers', when children had to rearrange the order of words 'make to sentence a meaningful'.

Now it's all Special Needs, and the children go to specially designated parts of the school which are always named after classic 'B' horror movies: The Link, The Sanctuary, The Transit Block.

Note to Junior Teachers: You are expected to be able to teach all the above, at any time and without warning. This is why you stand less chance of promotion than your Secondary colleague – because you aren't specialising.

Note to Supply Teachers: You are expected to be able to teach all the above, at any time, without warning, in any place, and without materials.

Current Educational Theories

We must return to the old educational theories.
– Everything is done much better abroad.
– Children should be streamed.
– Children should be unstreamed.
– Use of computers leads to greater literacy.
– Use of computers is a complete and utter waste of time and leads to a generation of total illiterates.
– Children learn best in small groups.
– Children learn best in enormous groups.
– Children should start school earlier.
– Children should start school later.
– Children should start school at the same age as now.
– Education should be more 'work orientated'.
– Education should be for leisure.

It should be quite clear from the above that the state of educational debate is extremely healthy and unlikely to contribute anything to educational advance for some time to come.

Local Management of Schools (LMS)

LMS is a most clever educational development. It means that schools now manage their own finances: paying teachers, buying books and equipment, budgeting for repairs, hiring the services of support staff and educational psychologists. Each school gets an annual slab of money and the Head decides how it is to be spent. Warmth? Pencils? Another teacher to lessen the pressures in every class? Inside lavatories?

The theory behind LMS is that, since no Heads have ever received any training in accountancy, business management or financial planning, they're the ideal people to take on this awesome responsibility. And LMS will make sure they don't waste their time dealing with the things they're supposed to know about, like education.

THE JOB

Education is like Ballroom Dancing: you're always moving to somebody else's tune and you're usually going in circles.

Lesson Preparation

Any senior professional whom you approach, plaintively bleating that you don't seem to be able to keep control, will bark back, "Are you preparing your lessons?" The answer must be "Yes" (unless you are hoping to be invalided out of teaching on grounds of insanity), but Lesson Preparation means different things to different people. Take your choice from:

Tinker. Turns up for each lesson with a variety of bits and pieces from which the children can select: photocopied worksheets, pictures to colour, blank outline maps. Is prepared for most emergencies.

Tailor. Turns up with a box of scissors and a hundred and one things to cut out. Lost without gum or glue stick. Is prepared for a few emergencies.

Soldier. Plans each lesson like a military campaign. Knows who sits where, sound on logistics, drills the children into conditioned and habitual responses. The sort of teacher who has chairs on tables right on the dot of home time, and whose class files out saying "Good Afternoon" politely. Doesn't have emergencies.

Sailor. Every lesson a mystery voyage, with the good ship 'Education' pounded by storms and driven hither and thither. An instinctive approach, based on the wildly optimistic notion that luck or inspiration will arrive just in the nick of time, like Columbus and the land bird, to quell the mutiny. Luck and inspiration usually don't. Every lesson is one long emergency, and many go to watery graves.

Rich Man. Most lessons start with the phrase: "Now, today I've brought along something new to show you." The something new could be a book, a jewel, an ostrich egg, a clockwork motor, a stone polishing machine, a stuffed squirrel – anything. Stock phrase: "If you can capture the children's interest at the outset…"

Poor Man. Has one basic textbook that he/she sticks with all year. A dull approach, but at least the children know what to expect. "Open your books and turn to the next exercise…"

Beggar Man. Attempts, pathetically, to get the children to do his or her work for him/her. "O.K., right, now – quieten down, please – O.K., right, today we're going – could you quieten down, please – today we're going to take a look at the work of the Police – O.K., O.K., O.K., come on, 3C, I've asked you to quieten down. Right. O.K. Now, I want you to give me some examples of what the Police do. No – I don't want you to shout things out like that – off the table, Lee – Now, come on, 3C, you know that's not the sort of thing I meant – where are you going, Carol? – I'm looking to you for ideas that I can write up on the board – but you must quieten down..."

Thief. Regularly nips into the staffroom or into other people's classrooms and grabs any good idea going. A very sound, common-sense approach. Problems arise only when the entire school is staffed with thieves.

Marking

Should you have been lucky enough to have obtained some work from your pupils, you are faced with the task of having to mark it. In general, follow the fashion of the day. Sometimes it's lots of red ink and comments in the margin and detailed criticisms and careful gradings and marks out of ten. Sometimes it's a huge tick at the bottom of the page, and an encouraging remark, such as 'Better'. This is a very useful comment, as it doesn't commit you to say how, or why, or better than what, yet it should please pupil, parent and Inspector.

A very simple way to handle all marking problems is to tick or correct the date, and then write: 'From now on I shall not mark any work that is not neatly presented, carefully punctuated and accurately spelt.' With luck you can go away for the next three or four weekends.

Reading Schemes and Tests

Every Reading Scheme is about two repugnant middle-class children, who live in a 1950s semi in what looks like Ruislip, and who have two odious parents locked in sexist roles. So many jokes have been made about this family and its ghastly pets that the subject has been virtually exhausted. Small wonder that so many children find the English language, difficult enough to learn to read in the first place, unattractive as a subject for their attention. A fortune awaits the genius who comes up with a Reading Scheme that features two really nasty, dirty, vicious little thugs, who murder their parents, set fire to the ancestral semi, do unmentionable things with Pat and Tibs, and bring riot and discredit to the whole of Acacia Villas.

Reading Tests similarly cling loyally to another age, containing words and phrases like 'woodman', 'milkman's horse', 'scythe', 'sepulchre' and 'almanac'. They might as well include 'liberty bodice', 'hansom', 'gentlemen's outfitter', and 'parlourmaid'. The worst offender is the Schonell 100, which sounds like a motor race, but is simply a printed list of 100 words, approximately 90 of which most adults are never likely to have to read ('homonym', 'judicature', 'sabre', 'somnambulist', 'bibliography'). Any child reading more than 20 words on this list has clearly been devilishly coached and learnt the list by heart.

Stock

One of the most important things a teacher has to learn is how to manage stock. Each school has its own system, some centralised – with a Head with Eyes as Big as Dinner Plates guarding the key – some departmentalised, so that you have to fill in a chitty to get what you want and you're never actually allowed into Aladdin's Cave.

Whatever the system, there has to be some way to short-circuit it, so that you can grab up to four times your share of books, paper, felt tips, paint, pencils, pens, rubbers (especially rubbers – no school stock cupboard ever has any rubbers between November and September), compasses, PVC glue, sellotape (almost as short a season as rubbers), scissors, slide binders, paper clips and box files (normally all gone in the first week of the Autumn term). The secret of being a good and successful teacher is having unlimited supplies. It's amazing what the promise of a new rubber will do to quieten even the most fractious pupil. How you achieve this *coup de provisions* is up to you. Some have tried getting hold of the key to the stock cupboard and making a quick plasticine impression. Others have favoured more direct action, using a Countdown card to slip back the deadlock. Some have gone too far, and involved the children and an entry through the back window.

The best approach is to arrive on the last weekday of the holidays. Chances are you will find the Schoolkeeper and his Alsatian surrounded by dozens of boxes of newly arrived stock. Offer to help him put them away, slipping Wotan a piece of drugged meat as you do so. Persist when the Schoolkeeper suspiciously spurns your offer. He'll crack when you point out it's near his dinner hour (12.15 – 2.45), and then you (and quantities of stock) are away.

Record Keeping

The purpose of Record Keeping is to make sure that teachers don't nip off at half past three every day, but you shouldn't resent this as it gives you a chance to daydream, to fantasise, to play 'Let's Pretend'. In Record Keeping, teachers write down:

- a) what was supposed to happen
- b) what they wish had happened
- c) what they know will never happen.

This is the creative writing side of Record Keeping. The other side is desperately trying to find sufficient information to fill six sides of A4 paper about a child of whom you have only the dimmest recollection. Can he blend sounds? Can she sort shapes? Has he seen the School Nurse? Can she draw the human body without putting the nose where the knee ought to be?

The only section on which you will be able to supply plenty of information will be the one that says: 'Does he/she present any particular management problems?' All children present particular management problems. The difficulty is to express your thoughts and findings without an ensuing libel action since School Records are now open documents. This is another example of the Perpetual Revolution in Teaching. It is clearly a great advance, with an interesting underground sideshoot. There are now secret files in many schools in which teachers write what they really think of the children, and feel a lot better for doing so.

Health and Safety

Probably the biggest disappointment in any teacher's career is when the team from the Architect's department comes round looking for asbestos and can't find any. Asbestos is much sought after in schools because its presence means the place has to be vacated for weeks and the whole system is thrown into chaos.

Most teachers are secretly delighted when the system is thrown into chaos. It means classes having to be cancelled or turning up late, or being moved to separate buildings, or – wonder of wonders – the school closing.

Health and Safety is really a very serious thing, and every school has a Health and Safety Rep. The Rep's job is:

1. To report everything that is wrong with the school to the Head (here disguised as the Key Manager) and the Schoolkeeper.
2. To wait 12 months while nothing is done.
3. To report everything that is wrong again.

Health and Safety Reps, therefore, lead very unfulfilled lives and tend to concentrate their energies on three things:

1. The temperature in classrooms. This is never right.
2. Hooks on the doors in corridors. This is an interesting and insoluble problem. If the doors are hooked back, there is no danger of children being banged in the face, but this will constitute a fire hazard as the doors are fire-retarding doors. The Health and Safety Rep thus has the choice of seeing his school burn down or be populated by toothless, broken-nosed children.
3. Holes in lino. A conscientious Health and Safety Rep counts and measures holes in lino and sends reports to the Education Office about them, which affords administrators the only laughs they get.

Assemblies

The Law says there must be a daily act of corporate worship in every school, but then the Law also says that you mustn't drive more than 30 miles an hour in a built-up area. In some form or another Ass-em-ber-ly (all four syllables should be equally stressed) survives in most schools. All you need to know is whether it is a One Man/Woman Show, or if there is a dreaded rota.

If the former, then it's a welcome break for the teachers: a chance to relax and daydream while the Head cajoles, harangues, presents swimming certificates and tells Warning Stories of the Dangers of Being a Non Swimmer, preaches, reads notices, reminisces and draws morals. If it's the latter, then sooner or later your time will come. You have to plan something. It's no good hoping there will be some awful catastrophe 'Somewhere' two days before, so that you can get your class to:

a) Show the school where 'Somewhere' is on the map
b) Give lurid details of the disaster
c) Explain how it would be a good idea if we all raised money for relief.

Because if there isn't a disaster, then you are stuck. Here, then, is a list of ideas* for Your Turn to Take Assembly:

> Our School 100 Years Ago*
> Anti-racism***
> Consideration for Others*
> Road Safety**
> Hegelian Concept of Historical Dialectic*
> The Eco System**
> The First Christmas/Easter/Ramadan/
>   Yom Kippur/Night of Power***
> Personal Cleanliness*
> A School Anti-litter Week***

* Rating: *Don't touch it **Worth a Try ***Good for prospects of promotion.

Make a mess of Assembly and you lose a tremendous amount of kudos. Do it well and the fatter, richer pay scales are almost within your grasp. Which brings us to:

Going for Promotion

There are teachers who sit back in the staffroom, gently fingering the tattoos on the backs of their hands and saying: "I mean, all this promotion crap. Who needs it? Working in the classroom with a bunch of kids. That's all what really matters. That's where it's at.* There's no way I'm prostituting myself for promotion." What they mean is, they have tried and failed. You have to try and succeed. There are two methods: the Tortoise and the Hare.

The Tortoise talks and dresses like a Head of Department or Deputy Head from the day he or she enters Training College, cultivates the Inspector, attends a lot of Courses and Meetings, produces Discussion Documents and Working Papers on How the Department Could be Streamlined, reads aloud bits of the *Times Ed.* in the staffroom, and (worst) is pleasant to everybody. By this method the Tortoise becomes universally hated in the school, and the Head feels obliged to give the Tortoise a glowing reference.

The Hare bounds through life in a merry and outrageously eccentric way, full of bon mots, witty epigrams and impossibly innovative ideas. By this method the Hare becomes universally hated in the school and the Head feels bound to give the Hare a glowing reference.

You then have to decide which of these methods to adopt and carry it through at interview. Here the Tortoise plods maddeningly along, wearing the interview

* Note the out-of-date argot: a feature of the Progressive.

panel down, remorselessly grinding them into acceptance of his or her solid professionalism. "We must have this teacher," is the panel's response, believing that the Tortoise will work assiduously for long hours and never put a foot wrong. The Hare's interview is livelier, a thing of fits and starts, leaving the panel bemused and divided. "Could be brilliant," say some. "Could be a disaster," say others. "Certainly different," say all. There is a chance that this 'difference' will swing the appointment in the Hare's favour.

The point about all this is that you need an alternative strategy if you find yourself competing with a whole lot of tortoises, or, less probably, hares. Don't look for a third successful method – there isn't one.

Going for a Headship

First, ask yourself "Why?" Why are you volunteering to take total responsibility for every single event that takes place in a school, probably the least controllable institution in the whole of our society? Think of what those events are likely to be: breakages, injuries, near riots, nervous breakdowns on a grand scale, blocked drains, thefts, supporting staff in industrial action while at the same time seeking to circumvent its effects, appeasing parents, bullying parents, calming visitors who have been insulted by children/the school-keeper/teacher/other visitors, justifying the school's catastrophic exam results.

There are those who protest that the great thing about getting a Headship is that you can impose your authority and personality on a school. This is rubbish, as many a staffroom will laughingly confirm. The only great thing about getting a Headship is that it means you don't have to seek anyone's permission to arrive late or leave early.

41

Staff Meetings

Staff Meetings are the Think Tank and Boilerhouse of every school. They start fifteen minutes after they are supposed to and are conducted either in bored silence, save for the Head's pathetic attempts to raise his or her staff to some level of feeble contribution, or else in an atmosphere of bitter animosity and blazing rancour. The silent meetings are for dealing with important subjects, like changes in examinations, curriculum, timetabling, streaming, fire drills, school uniform, the explosion in the Science Block. Rowdy, argumentative meetings are always about trivial matters – parking facilities, staff coffee (its continual disappearance) and who should do duty for absent teachers.

Meetings take the following form:

1. Introductory remarks by the Head, frequently inter-rupted by late comers who start boiling kettles, bleating for coffee, asking if anyone is supposed to be sitting in that chair, etc. In these introductory remarks the Head outlines those matters which (unfortunately) there wasn't time to discuss at the last meeting. This takes about 20 minutes.

2. Lengthy discussion of something that was not on the agenda but that one of the more argumentative members of staff has just thought of: 35 minutes.

3. Discussion of matters that should be discussed at this meeting but that (unfortunately) there will not now be time to discuss: a further ten minutes.

4. Fixing a time for the next meeting, at which matters that should have been discussed at this meeting but (unfortunately) weren't, can be discussed. This takes five minutes.

Staff meetings are, therefore, always at least one jump behind themselves. This ensures that humdrum, routine matters are not pushed aside by matters of real urgency or immediacy.

How to Survive Staff Meetings

You can try wearing an interested smile and a personal stereo, but most teachers fall back on older, deeper wisdoms. They join a clique. Every staffroom has cliques. There is the Union clique, the Anti-Union clique, the Multi-Ethnic clique, the Anti-Multi-Ethnic clique, the Let's Have the *Mirror/Socialist Worker/ Telegraph* in the Staffroom clique, the Anti-Let's Have the *Mirror*, etc.

This delicate balance of interests ensures that there is very little likelihood of anything ever happening in staffrooms. If you decide against joining a clique, cultivate a sardonic laugh. Sardonic laughs go a long way in education.

Unions

Teachers join unions for one of two reasons:

a) they are politically very, very, angry
b) they have just made a terrible professional mistake and can see an impending lawsuit racing towards them.

Whatever the reason, teachers have a choice. The **NUT** (National Union of Teachers) and the **NAS/ UWT** (National Association of Schoolmasters and Union of Women Teachers) have two purposes in life:
- to argue with each other (the politically very, very angry)

– to run protection rackets for teachers who freak out and smack children whose parents disapprove of that sort of thing (the impending lawsuit).

The **ATL** (Association of Teachers and Lecturers) has one purpose in life, which is to be as little like a trade union as possible. **PAT** (Professional Association of Teachers) has no purpose whatsoever, which is why it was set up.

The **NAHT** (National Association of Head Teachers) is the Bosses' Union, and meets once a year at a seaside resort (a different one each year as no resort will have them back) and makes Important Pronouncements on Educational Matters which are picked up by the Press but achieve nothing – just like all the other unions.

In questions of union affiliations, schools are rather like parliamentary constituencies: there are 'safe' NUT schools and 'safe' NAS/UWT schools. The majority of the profession takes little interest in Union matters and few attend meetings. This is a pity for Union meetings are second only to cremations when it comes to fun. To a newcomer they are quite incomprehensible, full of people bouncing up and down and demanding "On a point of *order*, Chair, on a *point of order*, that the Motion that the Motion be put, be referred back", and other people bouncing up and down and shouting that the meeting is not now 'quorate'. This is the desperate and secret desire of all present. What it means is that the pubs are open and members have nipped out.

Still others demand that "The Motion that the amendment be put, has been put, and you can't have a point of order". Then the Chair says it's time for fixed business and everything starts all over again.

Some people have suggested that Union Meetings are held to give teachers a chance to behave like naughty children and get their own back, but this seems like a gross distortion of the truth.

Disputes at School

From time to time, the stagnant calm that pervades education used to be shaken up by real, proper, grown-up disputes, and teachers went on strike. At such times you had to decide which you would rather be:

Conservative – The sort of fuddy-duddy who babbled about "putting the children first" and "taking a professional attitude", and didn't go on strike, but was happy to sit in the empty school writing a novel or repairing his car, and took every pay rise gained by strikes without batting an eyelid. Or,

Progressive – The sort of marcher and chanter who prattled about "class struggle" and "following in the footsteps of the Miners", and who thought that he had only to close the school for a couple of Wednesday afternoons and strut up and down with a cardboard placard saying 'Please Restore Pay Parity as Soon as It's Convenient' to bring about the collapse of the Stock Exchange and the imminent demise of the capitalist system.

Nowadays there aren't any strikes. This is because:

1. Teachers are no longer sure who employs them and, therefore, against whom the strike should be directed.

2. Teachers are so busy doing absolutely everything in their own classrooms they are unaware that there are other teachers employed in the school and that concerted action is possible.

3. Schools can no longer afford cardboard for the placards.

The Teaching Revolution

After dozing quietly for 40 years, education in Britain was rudely awakened by a succession of Education Secretaries, starting with Kenneth Baker and continuing with John Patten, Gillian Shephard and David Blunkett. The stated aim of the revolution was that education should become a true, working partnership. To which end:

1. Education has been removed from the hands of experts.

2. Teachers now have far less influence in education.

3. Parents now have far more influence in education, unless the DFEE think otherwise.

4. The DFEE always think otherwise.

From the mid 1980s to the late 1990s, directives burst forth weekly from the DFEE – urging, threatening, contradicting, promising, misleading, demanding, confusing. It was a truly wonderful time to be a teacher. And it was a true revolution in that it conformed to the worst excesses of the French Revolution, and we all know what that led to.

The Baker-Shephard Teaching Revolution led to:

1. Schools being allowed to opt out of LEA control if a simple majority of parents (or a majority of simple parents) so desired.

2. Schools no longer being burdened with resources – teachers, books, pencils, rooms, playing fields, etc.

3. Fewer teachers pretending to be suffering from stress. Nowadays, all teachers are genuinely suffering from stress.

4. Teachers being more efficient at teaching the wrong things to children who are no more efficient at learning them.

5. Teachers no longer complaining to their unions about pay and conditions, but more professional matters such as: "Why hasn't the NAS/UWT abolished bloodsports?", "What is the NUT doing about unemployment in Latvia?", "When will PAT restore capital punishment?"

Other triumphs of revolutionary planning included the idea that private business was longing to sponsor schools, and that everyone would enjoy daily Christian assemblies. When these plans were executed, the results were like all revolutionary executions – bloody and awful.

The Blunkett Revolution has accelerated this process and resulted in:

1. Fewer teachers complaining to their employers. Fewer teachers know who employs them.

2. Fewer teachers seeking early retirement in their 50s. Most teachers leave the profession in their 30s.

Covering Other Classes

Strikes may come and strikes may go, but teachers seem to have to face the problem of covering other classes for absent colleagues until the end of time. There are two ways to approach the problem:

Refuse, but in advance. A high moral stance works much better when the Head isn't facing a panic situation.

Accept. Show the Head you're happy to help out. Delight and surprise him/her. But have in your pocket a printed slip that reads: AM IN CLASS ... NO WORK SET. WITHDRAWING GOODWILL IN ... MINUTES.

Courses

Occasionally you will hear someone in the staffroom say: "I'm going on a course next week." If they are smiling, it means the course will be held during school hours. If they sound grimly resigned, it means the course is after school or at the weekend. If they go on to say something about "...leaving work set for classes..." it means they are rampant for promotion.

Although courses are organised by widely different bodies (University Extra Mural Departments, DFEE, LEAs, Voluntary Bodies, Open University, etc.), and have different titles ('A Diagnostic Approach to Table Tennis Skills', 'Whither Paired Reading?', 'Creative Writing and Appalling Behaviour – Is There a Connection?'), all courses are really exactly the same, and consist of four basic features:

1. **The Venue**
   A classroom with tables and chairs suitable for eight-year-olds.

2. **The Equipment**
   An overhead projector with a dried up set of pens and a badly scarred screen.

3. **The Personnel**
   Most of the people there will seem already to know each other, and will make quite a display of this, clapping each other on the back, giving the thumbs-up sign, nodding, waving, laughing uproariously while looking round, and generally doing all the things they cannot stand their pupils doing.

4. The Timetable

The day begins with **Lecture I**, given by an outsider ingratiatingly praised by the Course Leader. **Questions** are invited. There is one, asked by the Course Leader after an embarrassing silence. Much booze is consumed at **Lunchtime**. You will not have to face 3F with slurred speech and buckling knees.

Lecture II is given by a teacher who has oiled his or her way into favour. Listen to the first three minutes, which will reveal what pressures to expect from your Inspector, then go to sleep. Wake up for the **Group Discussion**, usually dominated by an Earnest Seeker After Truth, a Wag and a Malcontent. There is always the hope they will be brushed aside by a Nutcase – an engagingly demented character with a fund of mad ideas.

The day ends with **Conclusions and Recommendations** – the only reasonable conclusion being to recommend that such a thing never be repeated, especially once you realise you will clock off later than you would if you had stayed at school. Try not to let it affect the way you drive home.

Residential Courses. Similar to the Day Course (above), but with the added misery of knowing that you are going to have to spend an entire weekend with these people. Avoid sitting near the Wag at breakfast, or the Malcontent in the Bar, and beware the suggestion that: "We all meet up in a term's time to review progress."

Long Courses. These are altogether a different kettle of fish, especially if you are lucky enough to be seconded for a term or a year to attend some University or Institute of Education. Choose your course carefully – such opportunities occur only once in a teaching career.

Parents' Evenings/Open Days

Few Heads have been able to hold out successfully against the formation of **PTAs**, and lots of schools now adopt a kind of 'open house' approach to parents, inviting them into the classroom and even asking them to perform certain back-up tasks. Teachers may well support this, feeling that they don't see why they should have to suffer alone.

The result of all this is that parents are more to the fore, and much more knowledgeable about schools. They will arrive at Parents' Evenings with clear ideas in their heads as to what they want to discuss. What you have to do is master the special language by which parent and teacher communicate, e.g. Parent: "How's Chris getting on? Regular handful, I expect" (= I need reassuring that my child is doing well.) Teacher: "Not at all. Chris is beginning to settle down really well." (Chris is still fidgeting, dropping things and talking all the time.) This is what is called a Partnership in Education.

It's no good going mad and making the classroom lovely and triple mounting the children's artwork. One of the parents will be a member of Friends of the Earth, and you'll be treated to a 40-minute diatribe on deforestation and paper shortage. There are, however, a few points which make life easier:

1. Try to remember the names of the children you teach.

2. The night before, scribble a few red marks and comments around the books.

3. Have a strict timetable of visits clearly displayed on your desk so you can say to the Wellbeloveds or the Whinges, after they have spent 35 minutes blethering about the product of their loins, that you must attend to the next parent.

50

4. At the hour appointed for the evening to end, get up and switch off the lights. Even the Wellbeloveds find it hard to enthuse about their child in the dark.

5. It is not a bad idea to use such an occasion for one of your spasms of acute agony.

Visits

Visits are offered to pupils as treats, something out of the ordinary, a chance to have a nice time, something to shut them up for once, something to threaten to cancel if they don't behave.

Visits are hard to organise, costly in time and money, and throw burdens on to the rest of the school, whose precious timetable is disrupted. It seems a shame, therefore, that 95% of all educational visits are sources of deep unhappiness, frustration and bitterness. The main problems with visits are:

Public Transport – Too little, too late.

Public Conveniences – Too few, too far away.

The Public – Too unsympathetic.

Security Guards – Be it Hampton Court, Cheddar Gorge, Luton Airport, the Brontë Parsonage, St Ninian's Cave or the Ffestiniog Railway Museum – there are always Security Guards, men selected for their dislike and mistrust of children, and able to provoke at up to 300 metres.

Food – There can never be enough for children, who need to stuff themselves ceaselessly the moment they are removed from their natural habitat.

Control – It has been repeatedly proved that it is impossible to control children on any school visit.

Disregarding this last point, as all teachers do when they arrange visits, the best plan for a successful excursion would seem to be to walk your class to the nearest public loo, and lock them in with half a ton of sandwiches and some worksheets on Thomas Crapper.

Outings

These differ from Visits in one respect. Visits are supposed to be educational, outings are for pure fun. It is even more of a pity, therefore, that 95% of outings are also sources of deep unhappiness and frustration, and invariably lead to letters of complaint from Chambers of Commerce of seaside towns, Area Managers of British Rail, and Proprietors of Amusement Parks and Leisure Centres.

Some schools go so far as to arrange day trips abroad. This involves:

a) A frantic coachride to the coast during which the children sing silly songs, feel sick, giggle a lot and frequently need to visit the lavatory.
b) An arduous sea voyage across the Channel during which the children run dementedly round the boat deck, feel sick, have fights and lose things.
c) Four grisly hours in Calais or Boulogne during which the children buy inappropriate souvenirs (such as flick knives and packs of playing cards with nude pictures), refuse to sample the delicious local food and gorge themselves on chips and Coke, and come near to being arrested.
d) Another horrid Channel crossing during which the children loll around the fruit machines wishing they had some money left, *are* sick, and see to it that their teachers are given no time to enjoy the cheap booze in the bar.

e) Another frantic coachride back to school, during which...

The next day in Assembly, the Head asks to see all those who went on the outing, the flick knives and cards are confiscated, everyone is told off, and the teachers who went on the outing learn that it was a wonderfully quiet day at school.

School Journeys

These usually last a week, but it seems like much longer. On a school journey, a group of children are escorted by teachers, and all live together in a place that none of them would otherwise choose to go to. Nowadays school journeys are becoming more and more adventurous. Time was, a week on a Suffolk farm was sufficient. Now it's Battlefields of the Spanish Civil War, Mafia Outposts in Sicily, Transylvanian Ski Resorts, the Gulag Archipelago, and, more tamely, the Goodwin Sands.

Two types of teacher go on school journeys:

The Caring – who take things very seriously and diligently. They check all baggage, supervise every step the children take, deal with currency problems, encourage the children to use foreign tongues, comfort the sick and the neurotic, make sure everybody is warm, fed and labelled. They do everything possible to make sure the journey is a success and work themselves into the ground. Lots of things go wrong for them.

The Daring – who see a school journey as an opportunity to booze, gamble and fornicate their way round somewhere that is, at least, a sight more exotic than Warley, Merthyr Tydfil, Grantham or

Peebles. Blissfully ignoring the children, these teachers go all out for cirrhosis of the liver, obesity, bankruptcy and sexual exhaustion. In their own way they, too, do everything possible to make sure the journey is a success, and work themselves into the ground. Fewer things go wrong for them.

Take no notice of the apocryphal story of the teacher who took a skiing party to Switzerland and ended up on his own in a hotel for a fortnight, all expenses paid (after the others had returned home), while one of his charges recovered from peritonitis in a Swiss hospital. It's a wicked trick to make you volunteer, and you would be more likely to win the Irish Sweep.

The School Fête

This is held every year on the first wet Saturday in June. A gang of the merrier Dads dress comically, set up various stalls and have a lovely time pretending they are fairground barkers. Mums make dozens of fancy cakes and plates and plates of flapjacks, and there are plenty of other signs of failure of the school's Equal Opportunities Programme.

If the school is in an urban area there will be a stall selling Indian, West Indian, Greek or Turkish food. This will be delicious and will sell out long before anything else. There will be a fifth-hand book stall selling non-PC children's books, and an old clothes stall selling nothing. Some bright spark on the organising committee may well ask you to spend half an hour on the Aunty Sally where children can pelt you with wet sponges. Attendance at the fête is more or less compulsory, but only those riddled with masochism need go this far.

Concerts

Infant schools concerts are highly successful and much loved by all taking part and watching. Junior school concerts are distinguished by stage fright, lack of musical resources, lack of a musical specialist on the staff and repeated and unsuccessful attempts to stage *Joseph and the Amazing Technicolour Dreamcoat*. Secondary school concerts are distinguished by the Head of Music who conducts from the piano, counting very loudly in the hope that the performers will at least start together, mouthing each word hideously in the hope that they might stay together, and flailing his/her arms wildly in the hope that they will finish together. They won't.

How to Get Out of Teaching

There are six ways:

1. **Death**. This is not recommended, except in extreme cases, like teaching General Subjects in a Tory controlled urban area or any of the shires, and still being on the same salary after more than 20 years. In this case, death may come as a light relief.

2. **Early retirement**. This is the prize way out, and readily available at one time to all teachers over 30 with hardened arteries, soft brain cells, fallen arches, rising blood pressure and tennis elbow. This was in the good old days when LEAs realised it was cheaper to pension a teacher than employ one. These days LEAs haven't got the money to do either. You can try, but be prepared for sardonic laughter and bitter disappointment.

3. **Nervous Breakdown**. It is said that there is a 'struck-off' ex-Civil servant, a reject from the DFEE, who gives coaching in how to persuade tribunals you are having a nervous breakdown. It costs, and there is no offer of a 'No Fail – No Fee' arrangement. Nervous breakdowns used to be very popular in teaching, but, like the lob in tennis, they can be overplayed.

4. **Suspension**. Achieved in one of two ways – either physically maiming or politically indoctrinating a child. Worth a try as it can lead to at least a year off duties but on full pay while your case is being examined. Pick your child and/or your political theory carefully. Straight communism or Trotsky-ism won't do – it has got to be Baader-Meinhof, the Red Brigade, the INLA or the FCS.

5. **Slipping to the Side**. You could go for being an **ESW**, which is a dull but much quieter life, check-ing registers and driving school phobics to and fro at the Authority's expense. Or you could try being a **Careers Officer**, which is deadly dull and has even less chance of promotion than teaching, but where you can do everything by phone so that you never actually see a child at all.

6. **Opening a Wholefood Shop or Pottery**. Worth a try if you need to use your hands therapeutically, but watch your choice of location – they're full up in Blackheath, Dartington, Chichester, Maccles-field, Brecon, Wisbech, and every town in Cornwall and Perthshire.

GREAT NAMES IN EDUCATION

St Augustine who started the first R.E. classes in Britain.

Lord Baden-Powell who managed to persuade children to wear short trousers until Levis Strauss came along and persuaded them to wear jeans.

Enid Blyton who, although much maligned, has probably made more children want to read than any other person.

Rhodes Boyson who proved that lack of talent and looking odd need not prevent you becoming a Head.

Jerome Bruner who brilliantly showed that if eight teachers spend 20 hours a day with one child who has an IQ of 305, at the end of only six months that child can do simultaneous equations.

Mr Chips who showed that compulsory retirement is the best way of getting rid of boring old farts.

Froebel who taught that schools should be like gardens – a bit of mucking about, a bit of grassing, a few bo(a)rders and the whole thing fenced in.

The Jesuits who rightly pointed out that you can't do anything with a child once he or she has reached the age of eight.

A.S. Neill who showed that you can get children to run their own school so long as they have to cut their own firewood, draw their own water, cook their own food, make their own furniture, etc., so that they're always too exhausted to mess about.

Sir Isaac Pitman who invented the **ita** (initial teaching alphabet) which meant that children had to read Serbo-Croat before being allowed to go on to learn to read English.

Rousseau who was the first person to admit that children are like wild animals.

Wackford Squeers who was the first person to show that teachers are wild animals.

THE TEACHER'S YEAR

August (late): Single teachers return from Greece. Married teachers finish redecorating front room.

September: Academic Year begins. First signs of sore throats. Heads of Departments and above appear with new cars.

October: First staff discussions about doing something really different for Christmas this year.

November: Decision taken to "stick to what we did last Christmas" – hoop wrapped in metallic paper, rolled cardboard Three Wise Men, 'Lord of the Dance' and 'Figgy Pudding'.

December: Christmas Parties/Festivals/Concerts/Carol Services. Staff exhausted and full of ill will to all men and women. Letters arrive from bank revealing overdrawn accounts.

January: Disappointingly small snowfall. Staff still able to get to work. Equipment ordered last July arrives. Much searching of Jobs Abroad column in educational journals.

February: Single teachers leave for Half Term ski holiday in the Alps. Married teachers buy wallpaper stripper and lining paper.

March: March drop – many Fifth Years anticipate Statutory School Leaving Age. Many teachers profoundly grateful.

April: Easter leavers officially leave. Many Educational Psychologists, Heads and administrators profoundly grateful.

May: New football posts arrive. Whitsun leavers depart. Staff attendance improves.

June: Wimbledon fortnight. Staff absences rise.

July: Academic Year ends. Six weeks holiday begins. Teachers decide to stick it for another year.

GLOSSARY

The curriculum – A catch-all phrase that suggests some overall planning has gone into the weird menu the school offers its pupils.

Hidden curriculum – An excuse for not teaching the exposed curriculum.

Non contact time – Strictly, time out of the classroom to prepare or mark work. In reality, a chance to escape from the major drawback to teaching: children.

Integrated day – Not being able to keep to a timetable.

Extended day – Head's expression for sentencing teachers to Community Service.

GCSE – Latest in a long line of unsuccessful attempts to grade the school population in a form acceptable to bosses, elitists, socialists and the Civil Service.

Continuous assessment – Not being able to do end of term reports.

Self assessment – Making the children do their own marking.

Parental involvement – (1) Attempts to encourage uninterested parents in the workings of the school in the hope that they will back you up. (2) Attempts to control the nosey-parkering comings and goings of the same parents.

Warnock (or any other report) **implementation** – Attempts to justify some of the more bizarre recent innovations in the school.

New Maths – Totally outdated Maths.

Hands on experience – Attempts to justify children spending hours playing computer games of no educational value.

Split site – An excuse for having staff meetings during school hours and sending the children home early.

Four term year – A way for teachers to avoid the crush at campsites along the Loire in July and August.

Sanctions – Unsuccessful attempts to bring wild children to order, roughly the equivalent of telling a whirling Dervish to sit down nicely or he'll miss the first two minutes of break.

Child centred education – Attempts to justify LEGO, Monopoly, Snakes and Ladders, Colouring in, Poker, Noughts and Crosses, etc.

Capitation – A secret source of money known only to the Head, the School Secretary and the local Education Office; never enough to go round.

Falling rolls – An excuse for taking teachers away from schools just when the staffing ratio seems about right.

The bulge – An excuse for cramming 40 children in a classroom and telling the teacher to get on with it.

Tertiary education – An attempt to fudge the unemployment figures by keeping the virtually ineducable at school until they are 25.

Nuffield science – The name for all that unused equipment found at the back of the science cupboard.

Liaison and communication – The subjects of continual complaint by and about teachers who hold long meetings to communicate to each other how poor the level of communication between them is.

DFEE guidelines – The piles of unread pamphlets and circulars littering the staffroom until someone can stand it no longer and throws the lot away.

Open testimonial – A measuredly meaningless document that tells nobody anything about anybody.

Careers office – A place inhabited by ex-teachers who got out before they went under, but who pay for their escape by having to try to place up to 50 shiftless youths in the one vacancy available.

Inservice training – A morning, afternoon, day, or even week out of the trenches, resting behind lines and being talked at by Brass Hats.

Structure – Pathetic attempts by the Head to bring order to the chaos that rages through the school.

PTA – Six gloomy parents meeting in a gloomy room and making plans for the Summer Fête.

Plant utilisation – The Head of CDT servicing his car on school premises using school equipment, or any member of staff having a quick freebie on the telephone or photocopier.

Contracted in – A way of confusing women teachers, adopted by the Civil Service, and involving incomprehensible regulations about National Insurance.

Temporary terminal – A classification of teacher incomprehensible to the pay clerk at the Education Office and all other administrators, and whose contract arrives for acceptance three weeks after it expires.

Late starter – Desperately stupid but large child.

Slow developer – Desperately stupid child who is still growing.

Specific learning difficulties – An excuse for not being able to teach a child any particular part of the educational syllabus – reading, numeracy, tying shoelaces, standing up without hitting somebody, differential calculus, etc.

ESW (Educational Social Worker) – Truant officer without any power, effect, respect or affection.

TEFL – Teaching English as if it was a foreign language.

Dyslexia – Spelling English as if it was a foreign language.

Multi-disciplinary – Total lack of communication between teachers, social workers, psychiatrists, child care staff, psychologists, Juvenile Bureau officers and ESWs achieved through many lengthy case conferences where nobody can remember who anybody is, or even which case is being conferenced.

League Tables – Published lists of performance which take no account of variations in pupil intake, pupil–teacher ratios, pupil ability, or any other likely influences on the results. Teachers hate them, pupils aren't interested, educationalists doubt their validity, but governments love them because they appear to do that which had formerly been thought impossible, i.e. judge how well or badly teachers perform. And this has paved the way for the greatest educational reform of all time: paying some teachers less.

Nashnull Litressee Straterjee – A Guvment backd skeme to inhanse the teechin of wreedin and wrightin and grammer by havvin evreewun do an huor a day wreedin and wrightin and grammerin.

Initials

Like the New Year's Day Honours List, education now consists largely of initials. Some are old favourites, like HM, EO, JMI and VSOP, but a whole set of new ones has come along:

KS 1, **KS 2**, **KS 3** – The Key Stages in education, reckoned to be 7, 11 and 14 years, at which **SATS** (Standard Assessment Tasks) are applied. Cornerstones of this innovation are the twin educational notions: a) it is more useful to test than to teach; b) it is more acceptable to fail than to learn.

GEST – Grants for Educational Support and Training. LSD from the DFEE for, say, vocational courses so that those who fail their GCSEs won't necessarily end up in HMPs.

TVEI – Training and Vocational Education Initiatives. Basically indistinguishable from GEST, except that the main purpose of TVEI is to find something to occupy any inspectors that are left.

PRP – Performance Related Pay, the 1990s equivalent of the Victorian PBR (Payment by Results).

Ofsted – Office of Standards in Education. It's a sort of watchdog (*cf.* Oftel, Ofgas), a body that has replaced the previous state and LEA inspectorate, and probably as toothless. There are those teachers who say the initials stand for **Oh For Something That Ends Drudgery**. Some hope.

THE AUTHOR

Nick Yapp first went to a little school run by Miss Wills and Miss Fuller, who were nice and kind and didn't hit anybody. Then he went to a bigger school run by Mr Springman, who was cruel and sadistic and hit everybody. Then he went to a much bigger school, for big boys, where everybody hit everybody.

By failing exams he took so long to get a degree in Law he avoided National Service. After that he taught in a variety of schools before moving to Special Education. From 1971 to 1979, with a year off to get an MA in Child Development, he taught in a school for maladjusted children. In 1980 he became Head of another maladjusted school, but resigned ten months later because he couldn't stand the Deputy Head, the DFEE inspector, and the fact that the Schoolkeeper's dog was called 'Nigger'.

He returned to his previous school in 1981, and since then has gradually moved out of teaching into writing, slipping joyfully backwards down the promotional ladder with delightful ease.

His interests are music, cooking and cricket, and his ambitions are to visit dozens of countries and to make Catford the Cultural Centre of Western Europe. Both may take a little time.

He receives tremendous help and encouragement from his wife and children, all of whom he loves in a somewhat soppy fashion.